Scarves & Cowls

Reflect your personal style with scarves and cowls in custom widths and lengths! Complete instructions are given for the 12 projects shown inside. Plus, easy-to-follow charts are your guide to dozens more sizes. The options are endless!

4

8

12

16

20

24

LEISURE ARTS, INC. • Maumelle, Arkansas

Karen Ratto-Whooley

Karen Ratto-Whooley says childhood crochet lessons from her Italian grandmother helped her become the designer that she is today. "She didn't speak English, so she didn't know how to read an American pattern," Karen explains. "She taught me how to 'read the pictures' in order to create the item in the book. Because of this, I tended to make patterns differently than they were written, because many times I had to figure out how it was put together. So technically I consider myself a designer from the age of 7!"

Karen's designs for knitting, crochet, and the Knook have been published in numerous books and magazines, and she teaches nationwide at special events and in classes at guilds and yarn shops. A self-described "computer geek at heart," she does her own web design and marketing for her indie pattern line, KRW Knitwear Studio.

For more about Karen, visit her website, www.KRWknitwear.com.

How to Use This Book:

Each of the six designs in this book is shown in two sizes, as a scarf and a cowl. Complete instructions are provided for making the photographed models, so you don't have to change a thing to come out with wonderful results.

To give you more options, we've already done the math for numerous sizes of each design. Easy-to-follow charts list the measurements for each size, the skeins of yarn needed, and the stitch count for casting on.

On the facing page, you can see our two variations of the Cables design from pages 12-15. Notice how the same pattern and yarn has been used to produce a 4" wide scarf and a 5¾" tall cowl.

Besides varying the sizes, you also can change up the look of each design with your yarn choice. Look for different textures, choose between solid versus variegated colors, or pick novelty yarns with special effects such as sequins.

Six designs, with 8 sizes for each scarf and 8 sizes for each cowl, gives you a total of 96 pre-planned variations in this book. Just in case you still don't find the size you want, we've also provided instructions for how to calculate larger or smaller sizes, using the pattern Multiple (see page 30).

Creating a scarf or cowl that is exactly what you want has never been easier. Just imagine all the possibilities!

WE'VE DONE THE MATH FOR YOU!

Just choose the size you want from our easy-to-follow charts, such as these examples from the Cables design on pages 12-15.

Size (inches)	Size (centimeters)	Skein(s) Needed	Cast on
3 x 54	7.5 x 137	1	22

Size (inches)	Size (centimeters)	Skein(s) Needed	Cast on
4½ x 40	11.5 x 101.5	1	32

CUSTOMIZE YOUR SCARF

Multiple of 5 + 2 (see Multiples, page 30)

Choose a size below, cast on the required number of stitches, then follow the instructions for the pattern until your Scarf measures the desired length. The yarn needed for each size is based on getting the specified gauge with a Light Weight yarn with 282 yards (258 meters) per skein.

Size (inches)	Size (centimeters)	Skein(s) Needed	Cast on
3 x 40	7.5 x 101.5	1	22
3 x 54	7.5 x 137	1	22
3 x 60	7.5 x 152.5	1	22
4½ x 40	11.5 x 101.5	1	32
4½ x 54	11.5 x 137	2	32
4½ x 60	11.5 x 152.5	2	32
8 x 40	20.5 x 101.5	2	57
8 x 54	20.5 x 137	2	57

CUSTOMIZE YOUR COWL

Multiple of 5 + 2 (see Multiples, page 30)

Choose a size below, cast on the required number of stitches, then follow the instructions for the pattern until your Cowl measures the desired circumference. The yarn needed for each size is based on getting the specified gauge with a Light Weight yarn with 282 yards (258 meters) per skein.

Size (inches)	Size (centimeters)	Skein(s) Needed	Cast on
3 x 28	7.5 x 71	1	22
3 x 40	7.5 x 101.5	1	22
4½ x 28	11.5 x 71	1	32
4½ x 40	11.5 x 101.5	1	32
8 x 28	20.5 x 71	1	57
8 x 40	20.5 x 101.5	2	57
9½ x 28	24 x 71	2	67
9½ x 40	24 x 101.5	2	67

Ribbed

 **EASY**

SHOPPING LIST

Yarn (Super Bulky Weight)

[3.5 ounces, 90 yards (100 grams, 82 meters) per skein]:

Scarf

☐ 3 skeins

Cowl

☐ 3 skeins

Knitting Needle

36" (91.5 cm) Circular needle,

☐ Size 15 (10 mm) **or** size needed for gauge

Additional Supplies

☐ Yarn needle (for sewing Cowl)

SIZE INFORMATION

Scarf - 6" wide x 60" long

(15 cm x 152.5 cm) (after blocking)

Cowl - 10" tall x 40" circumference

(25.5 cm x 101.5 cm) (after blocking)

GAUGE INFORMATION

In pattern, 12 sts and 20 rows = 4" (10 cm)

Each row is worked across the length of the piece. The Scarf has a different multiple that allows for 3 knit stitches to be worked at each end to make a nicer finished edge.

INSTRUCTIONS
Scarf

Cast on 181 sts.

Row 1: K3, with yarn in **back**, slip 1 as if to **purl**, ★ with yarn in **front**, P1, with yarn in **back**, slip 1 as if to **purl**; repeat from ★ across to last 3 sts, K3.

Row 2: K3, purl across to last 3 sts, K3.

Repeat Rows 1 and 2 for pattern until Scarf measures approximately 6" (15 cm) from cast on edge, ending by working Row 1.

Bind off all sts in pattern.

Block Scarf *(see Blocking, page 31).*

Cowl

Cast on 120 sts.

Row 1 (Right side)**:** ★ With yarn in **back**, slip 1 as if to **purl**, with yarn in **front**, P1; repeat from ★ across.

Row 2: Purl across.

Repeat Rows 1 and 2 for pattern until Cowl measures approximately 10" (25.5 cm) from cast on edge, ending by working Row 1.

Bind off all sts in pattern, leaving a long end for sewing.

Block Cowl *(see Blocking, page 31).*

With **right** side together, sew short ends of Cowl together. For a Mobius, twist the strip once so that **wrong** and **right** sides are together, then sew short ends together.

CUSTOMIZE YOUR SCARF

Multiple of 2 + 1 *(see Multiples, page 30)*
Choose a size below, cast on the required number of stitches, then follow the instructions for the pattern until the Scarf measures the desired width. The yarn needed for each size is based on getting the specified gauge with a Super Bulky Weight yarn with 90 yards (82 meters) per skein.

Size (inches)	Size (centimeters)	Skein(s) Needed	Cast on
4 x 40	10 x 101.5	2	121
4 x 55	10 x 139.5	2	165
4 x 60	10 x 152.5	2	181
6 x 40	15 x 101.5	2	121
6 x 55	15 x 139.5	3	165
6 x 60	15 x 152.5	3	181
10 x 40	25.5 x 101.5	3	121
10 x 55	25.5 x 139.5	4	165

CUSTOMIZE YOUR COWL

Multiple of 2 *(see Multiples, page 30)*
Choose a size below, cast on the required number of stitches, then follow the instructions for the pattern until the Cowl measures the desired height. The yarn needed for each size is based on getting the specified gauge with a Super Bulky Weight yarn with 90 yards (82 meters) per skein.

Size (inches)	Size (centimeters)	Skein(s) Needed	Cast on
4 x 28	10 x 71	1	86
4 x 40	10 x 101.5	2	120
6 x 28	15 x 71	2	86
6 x 40	15 x 101.5	2	120
10 x 28	25.5 x 71	2	86
10 x 40	25.5 x 101.5	3	120
12 x 28	30.5 x 71	3	86
12 x 40	30.5 x 101.5	4	120

Pebbles

EASY

SIZE INFORMATION

Scarf - 5½" wide x 60" long
(14 cm x 152.5 cm)

Cowl - 9½" tall x 28" circumference
(24 cm x 71 cm)

GAUGE INFORMATION

In pattern, 22 sts and 24 rows = 4" (10 cm)

INSTRUCTIONS
Scarf

Cast on 31 sts.

Row 1: P1, (K1, P1) across.

Row 2: K1, ★ with yarn in **front**, slip 1 as if to **purl**, K1; repeat from ★ across.

Row 3: K1, (P1, K1) across.

Row 4: K2, ★ with yarn in **front**, slip 1 as if to **purl**, K1; repeat from ★ across to last 3 sts, with yarn in **front**, slip 1 as if to **purl**, K2.

Repeat Rows 1-4 for pattern until Scarf measures approximately 60" (152.5 cm) from cast on edge, ending by working Row 2 or 4.

Bind off all sts in pattern.

Block Scarf *(see Blocking, page 31)*.

Cowl

Cast on 53 sts.

Row 1: P1, (K1, P1) across.

Row 2 (Right side)**:** K1, ★ with yarn in **front**, slip 1 as if to **purl**, K1; repeat from ★ across.

Row 3: K1, (P1, K1) across.

Row 4: K2, ★ with yarn in **front**, slip 1 as if to **purl**, K1; repeat from ★ across to last 3 sts, with yarn in **front**, slip 1 as if to **purl**, K2.

Repeat Rows 1-4 for pattern until Cowl measures approximately 28" (71 cm) from cast on edge, ending by working Row 2 or 4.

Bind off all sts in pattern, leaving a long end for sewing.

Block Cowl *(see Blocking, page 31)*.

With **right** side together, sew short ends of Cowl together. For a Mobius, twist the strip once so that **wrong** and **right** sides are together, then sew short ends together.

CUSTOMIZE YOUR SCARF

Multiple of 2 + 1 *(see Multiples, page 30)*
Choose a size below, cast on the required number of stitches, then follow the instructions for the pattern until the Scarf measures the desired length. The yarn needed for each size is based on getting the specified gauge with a Fine Weight yarn with 99 yards (90 meters) per skein.

Size (inches)	Size (centimeters)	Skein(s) Needed	Cast on
3¾ x 40	9.5 x 101.5	2	21
3¾ x 54	9.5 x 137	2	21
3¾ x 60	9.5 x 152.5	2	21
5½ x 40	14 x 101.5	2	31
5½ x 54	14 x 137	3	31
5½ x 60	14 x 152.5	3	31
9½ x 40	24 x 101.5	4	53
9½ x 54	24 x 137	5	53

CUSTOMIZE YOUR COWL

Multiple of 2 + 1 *(see Multiples, page 30)*
Choose a size below, cast on the required number of stitches, then follow the instructions for the pattern until the Cowl measures the desired circumference. The yarn needed for each size is based on getting the specified gauge with a Fine Weight yarn with 99 yards (90 meters) per skein.

Size (inches)	Size (centimeters)	Skein(s) Needed	Cast on
3¾ x 28	9.5 x 71	1	21
3¾ x 40	9.5 x 101.5	2	21
5½ x 28	14 x 71	2	31
5½ x 40	14 x 101.5	2	31
9½ x 28	24 x 71	3	53
9½ x 40	24 x 101.5	4	53
11¾ x 28	30 x 71	3	65
11¾ x 40	30 x 101.5	4	65

Cables

■■□□ **EASY**

SHOPPING LIST

Yarn (Light Weight)
[2.4 ounces, 282 yards (70 grams, 258 meters) per skein]:

Scarf

☐ 1 skein

Cowl

☐ 1 skein

Knitting Needles

Straight,

☐ Size 6 (4 mm) **or** size needed for gauge

Additional Supplies

☐ Cable needle

☐ Tapestry needle (for sewing Cowl)

SIZE INFORMATION

Scarf - 3" wide x 54" long

(7.5 cm x 137 cm) (after blocking)

Cowl - 4½" tall x 40" circumference

(11.5 cm x 101.5 cm)

(after blocking)

GAUGE INFORMATION

In pattern, 15 sts (3 Cables) = 2" (5 cm)

(after blocking)

STITCH GUIDE

CABLE 4 BACK *(abbreviated C4B)*
Slip next 2 sts onto cable needle and
hold in **back** of work, K2 from left
needle, K2 from cable needle.

INSTRUCTIONS
Scarf

Cast on 22 sts.

Row 1: K3, P1, ★ K4, P1; repeat from
★ across to last 3 sts, K3.

Row 2: K4, P4, ★ K1, P4; repeat from ★
across to last 4 sts, K4.

Rows 3 and 4: Repeat Rows 1 and 2.

Row 5: K3, P1, ★ work C4B, P1; repeat
from ★ across to last 3 sts, K3.

Row 6: K4, P4, ★ K1, P4; repeat from ★
across to last 4 sts, K4.

Repeat Rows 1-6 for pattern until
Scarf measures approximately 54"
(137 cm) from cast on edge, ending
by working Row 3.

Bind off all sts in pattern.

Block Scarf *(see Blocking, page 31)*.

Cowl

Cast on 32 sts.

Row 1 (Right side): K3, P1, ★ K4, P1; repeat from ★ across to last 3 sts, K3.

Row 2: K4, P4, ★ K1, P4; repeat from ★ across to last 4 sts, K4.

Rows 3 and 4: Repeat Rows 1 and 2.

Row 5: K3, P1, ★ work C4B, P1; repeat from ★ across to last 3 sts, K3.

Row 6: K4, P4, ★ K1, P4; repeat from ★ across to last 4 sts, K4.

Repeat Rows 1-6 for pattern until Cowl measures approximately 40" (101.5 cm) from cast on edge, ending by working Row 3.

Bind off all sts in pattern, leaving a long end for sewing.

Block Cowl (*see Blocking, page 31*).

With **right** side together, sew short ends of Cowl together.

CUSTOMIZE YOUR SCARF

Multiple of 5 + 2 (*see Multiples, page 30*)
Choose a size below, cast on the required number of stitches, then follow the instructions for the pattern until your Scarf measures the desired length. The yarn needed for each size is based on getting the specified gauge with a Light Weight yarn with 282 yards (258 meters) per skein.

Size (inches)	Size (centimeters)	Skein(s) Needed	Cast on
3 x 40	7.5 x 101.5	1	22
3 x 54	7.5 x 137	1	22
3 x 60	7.5 x 152.5	1	22
4½ x 40	11.5 x 101.5	1	32
4½ x 54	11.5 x 137	2	32
4½ x 60	11.5 x 152.5	2	32
8 x 40	20.5 x 101.5	2	57
8 x 54	20.5 x 137	2	57

CUSTOMIZE YOUR COWL

Multiple of 5 + 2 (*see Multiples, page 30*)
Choose a size below, cast on the required number of stitches, then follow the instructions for the pattern until your Cowl measures the desired circumference. The yarn needed for each size is based on getting the specified gauge with a Light Weight yarn with 282 yards (258 meters) per skein.

Size (inches)	Size (centimeters)	Skein(s) Needed	Cast on
3 x 28	7.5 x 71	1	22
3 x 40	7.5 x 101.5	1	22
4½ x 28	11.5 x 71	1	32
4½ x 40	11.5 x 101.5	1	32
8 x 28	20.5 x 71	1	57
8 x 40	20.5 x 101.5	2	57
9½ x 28	24 x 71	2	67
9½ x 40	24 x 101.5	2	67

Clover

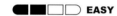 **EASY**

SHOPPING LIST

Yarn (Medium Weight)

[3.5 ounces, 151 yards (100 grams, 138 meters) per skein]:

Scarf

☐ 2 skeins

Cowl

☐ 2 skeins

Knitting Needles

Straight,

☐ Size 10½ (6.5 mm) **or** size needed for gauge

Additional Supplies

☐ Yarn needle (for sewing Cowl)

SIZE INFORMATION

Scarf - 4½" wide x 54" long

    (11.5 cm x 137 cm) (after blocking)

Cowl - 10" tall x 28" circumference

    (25.5 cm x 71 cm) (after blocking)

GAUGE INFORMATION

In pattern,

    18 sts and 20 rows = 4" (10 cm)

TECHNIQUES USED

- P2 tog (*Fig. 2, page 30*)
- Slip 1 as if to **knit**, K1, PSSO (*Fig. 3, page 30*)
- Slip 1 as if to **knit**, K2 tog, PSSO (*Fig. 4, page 31*)
- YO (*Figs. 5a & b, page 31*)

INSTRUCTIONS
Scarf

Cast on 21 sts.

Row 1: K3, ★ YO, slip 1 as if to **knit**, K2 tog, PSSO, YO, K3; repeat from ★ across.

Row 2: P2, P2 tog, YO, P1, YO, P2 tog, ★ P1, P2 tog, YO, P1, YO, P2 tog; repeat from ★ across to last 2 sts, P2.

Row 3: K1, K2 tog, YO, K3, ★ YO, slip 1 as if to **knit**, K2 tog, PSSO, YO, K3; repeat from ★ across to last 3 sts, YO, slip 1 as if to **knit**, K1, PSSO, K1.

Row 4: P2, YO, P2 tog, P1, P2 tog, ★ YO, P1, YO, P2 tog, P1, P2 tog; repeat from ★ across to last 2 sts, YO, P2.

Repeat Rows 1-4 for pattern until Scarf measures approximately 54" (137 cm) from cast on edge, ending by working Row 3.

Bind off all sts in pattern.

Block Scarf (*see Blocking, page 31*).

Cowl

Cast on 45 sts.

Row 1 (Right side)**:** K3, ★ YO, slip 1 as if to **knit**, K2 tog, PSSO, YO, K3; repeat from ★ across.

Row 2: P2, P2 tog, YO, P1, YO, P2 tog, ★ P1, P2 tog, YO, P1, YO, P2 tog; repeat from ★ across to last 2 sts, P2.

Row 3: K1, K2 tog, YO, K3, ★ YO, slip 1 as if to **knit**, K2 tog, PSSO, YO, K3; repeat from ★ across to last 3 sts, YO, slip 1 as if to **knit**, K1, PSSO, K1.

Row 4: P2, YO, P2 tog, P1, P2 tog, ★ YO, P1, YO, P2 tog, P1, P2 tog; repeat from ★ across to last 2 sts, YO, P2.

Repeat Rows 1-4 for pattern until Cowl measures approximately 28" (71 cm) from cast on edge, ending by working Row 3.

Bind off all sts in pattern, leaving a long end for sewing.

Block Cowl *(see Blocking, page 31).*

With **right** side together, sew short ends of Cowl together. For a Mobius, twist the strip once so that **wrong** and **right** sides are together, then sew short ends together.

CUSTOMIZE YOUR SCARF

Multiple of 6 + 3 *(see Multiples, page 30)*
Choose a size below, cast on the required number of stitches, then follow the instructions for the pattern until the Scarf measures the desired length. The yarn needed for each size is based on getting the specified gauge with a Medium Weight yarn with 151 yards (138 meters) per skein.

Size (inches)	Size (centimeters)	Skein(s) Needed	Cast on
4½ x 40	11.5 x 101.5	1	21
4½ x 54	11.5 x 137	2	21
4½ x 60	11.5 x 152.5	2	21
6 x 40	15 x 101.5	2	27
6 x 54	15 x 137	2	27
6 x 60	15 x 152.5	2	27
10 x 40	25.5 x 101.5	2	45
10 x 54	25.5 x 137	3	45

CUSTOMIZE YOUR COWL

Multiple of 6 + 3 *(see Multiples, page 30)*
Choose a size below, cast on the required number of stitches, then follow the instructions for the pattern until the Cowl measures the desired circumference. The yarn needed for each size is based on getting the specified gauge with a Medium Weight yarn with 151 yards (138 meters) per skein.

Size (inches)	Size (centimeters)	Skein(s) Needed	Cast on
4½ x 28	11.5 x 71	1	21
4½ x 40	11.5 x 101.5	1	21
6 x 28	15 x 71	1	27
6 x 40	15 x 101.5	2	27
10 x 28	25.5 x 71	2	45
10 x 40	25.5 x 101.5	2	45
12½ x 28	32 x 71	2	57
12½ x 40	32 x 101.5	3	57

Half Linen

 **EASY**

SIZE INFORMATION

Scarf - 4" wide x 54" long

(10 cm x 137 cm) (after blocking)

Cowl - 6" tall x 40" circumference

(15 cm x 101.5 cm) (after blocking)

GAUGE INFORMATION

In Stockinette Stitch

(knit one row, purl one row)

holding two strands of yarn together,

20 sts and 24 rows = 4" (10 cm)

INSTRUCTIONS
Scarf

Holding two strands of yarn together, cast on 19 sts.

Row 1: Knit across.

Row 2: K1, ★ with yarn in **front**, slip 1 as if to **purl**, with yarn in **back**, K1; repeat from ★ across.

Row 3: Purl across.

Row 4: K2, with yarn in **front**, slip 1 as if to **purl**, ★ with yarn in **back**, K1, with yarn in **front**, slip 1 as if to **purl**; repeat from ★ across to last 2 sts, with yarn in **back**, K2.

Row 5: Purl across.

Repeat Rows 2-5 for pattern until Scarf measures approximately 54" (137 cm) from cast on edge, ending by working Row 4.

Bind off all sts in **purl**.

Block Scarf *(see Blocking, page 31).*

Cowl

Holding two strands of yarn together, cast on 29 sts.

Row 1: Knit across.

Row 2 (Right side)**:** K1, ★ with yarn in **front**, slip 1 as if to **purl**, with yarn in **back**, K1; repeat from ★ across.

Row 3: Purl across.

Row 4: K2, with yarn in **front**, slip 1 as if to **purl**, ★ with yarn in **back**, K1, with yarn in **front**, slip 1 as if to **purl**; repeat from ★ across to last 2 sts, with yarn in **back**, K2.

Row 5: Purl across.

Repeat Rows 2-5 for pattern until Cowl measures approximately 40" (101.5 cm) from cast on edge, ending by working Row 4.

Bind off all sts in **purl**, leaving a long end for sewing.

Block Cowl *(see Blocking, page 31).*

With **right** side together, sew short ends of Cowl together. For a Mobius, twist the strip once so that **wrong** and **right** sides are together, then sew short ends together.

CUSTOMIZE YOUR SCARF

Multiple of 2 + 1 *(see Multiples, page 30)*
Choose a size below, cast on the required number of stitches, then follow the instructions for the pattern until the Scarf measures the desired length. The yarn needed for each size is based on getting the specified gauge with a Super Fine Weight yarn worked with double strands and with 230 yards (210 meters) per skein.

Size (inches)	Size (centimeters)	Skein(s) Needed	Cast on
4 x 40	10 x 101.5	2	19
4 x 54	10 x 137	2	19
4 x 60	10 x 152.5	2	19
6 x 40	15 x 101.5	2	29
6 x 54	15 x 137	3	29
6 x 60	15 x 152.5	3	29
10 x 40	25.5 x 101.5	3	49
10 x 54	25.5 x 137	4	49

CUSTOMIZE YOUR COWL

Multiple of 2 + 1 *(see Multiples, page 30)*
Choose a size below, cast on the required number of stitches, then follow the instructions for the pattern until the Cowl measures the desired circumference. The yarn needed for each size is based on getting the specified gauge with a Super Fine Weight yarn worked with double strands and with 230 yards (210 meters) per skein.

Size (inches)	Size (centimeters)	Skein(s) Needed	Cast on
4 x 28	10 x 71	1	19
4 x 40	10 x 101.5	2	19
6 x 28	15 x 71	2	29
6 x 40	15 x 101.5	2	29
10 x 28	25.5 x 71	2	49
10 x 40	25.5 x 101.5	3	49
12 x 28	30.5 x 71	3	59
12 x 40	30.5 x 101.5	4	59

Zig Zag

⬤⬛⬛⬛▢ **INTERMEDIATE**

SHOPPING LIST

Yarn (Medium Weight)
[4 ounces, 208 yards (113 grams, 190 meters) per skein]:

Scarf

☐ 2 skeins

Cowl

☐ 1 skein

Knitting Needles

Straight,

☐ Size 9 (5.5 mm) **or** size needed for gauge

Additional Supplies

☐ Yarn needle (for sewing Cowl)

SIZE INFORMATION

Scarf - 10¼" wide x 54" long

(26 cm x 137 cm)

Cowl - 5¾" tall x 40" circumference

(14.5 cm x 101.5 cm)

GAUGE INFORMATION

In Stockinette Stitch

(knit one row, purl one row),

18 sts and 24 rows = 4" (10 cm)

TECHNIQUES USED

K2 tog (*Fig. 1, page 30*)

Slip 1 as if to **knit**, K1, PSSO

  (*Fig. 3, page 30*)

YO (*Figs. 5c & d, page 31*)

INSTRUCTIONS
Scarf

Cast on 46 sts.

Row 1: P3, K2 tog, ★ YO, P3, K2 tog; repeat from ★ across to last st, YO, P1.

Row 2: K2, P1, (K4, P1) across to last 3 sts, K3.

Row 3: P2, K2 tog, ★ YO, P3, K2 tog; repeat from ★ across to last 2 sts, YO, P2.

Row 4: K3, P1, (K4, P1) across to last 2 sts, K2.

Row 5: P1, ★ K2 tog, YO, P3; repeat from ★ across.

Row 6: (K4, P1) across to last st, K1.

Row 7: P1, ★ YO, slip 1 as if to **knit**, K1, PSSO, P3; repeat from ★ across.

Row 8: K3, P1, (K4, P1) across to last 2 sts, K2.

Row 9: P2, YO, slip 1 as if to **knit**, K1, PSSO, ★ P3, YO, slip 1 as if to **knit**, K1, PSSO; repeat from ★ across to last 2 sts, P2.

Row 10: K2, P1, (K4, P1) across to last 3 sts, K3.

Row 11: ★ P3, YO, slip 1 as if to **knit**, K1, PSSO; repeat from ★ across to last st, P1.

Row 12: K1, (P1, K4) across.

Repeat Rows 1-12 for pattern until Scarf measures approximately 54" (137 cm) from cast on edge, ending by working Row 11.

Bind off all sts in pattern.

Block Scarf (*see Blocking, page 31*).

Cowl

Cast on 26 sts.

Row 1 (Right side)**:** P3, K2 tog, ★ YO, P3, K2 tog; repeat from ★ across to last st, YO, P1.

Row 2: K2, P1, (K4, P1) across to last 3 sts, K3.

Row 3: P2, K2 tog, ★ YO, P3, K2 tog; repeat from ★ across to last 2 sts, YO, P2.

Row 4: K3, P1, (K4, P1) across to last 2 sts, K2.

Row 5: P1, ★ K2 tog, YO, P3; repeat from ★ across.

Row 6: (K4, P1) across to last st, K1.

Row 7: P1, ★ YO, slip 1 as if to **knit**, K1, PSSO, P3; repeat from ★ across.

Row 8: K3, P1, ★ K4, P1; repeat from ★ across to last 2 sts, K2.

■□□□ BEGINNER	Projects for first-time knitters using basic knit and purl stitches. Minimal shaping.
■■□□ EASY	Projects using basic stitches, repetitive stitch patterns, simple color changes, and simple shaping and finishing.
■■■□ INTERMEDIATE	Projects with a variety of stitches, such as basic cables and lace, simple intarsia, double-pointed needles and knitting in the round needle techniques, mid-level shaping and finishing.
■■■■ EXPERIENCED	Projects using advanced techniques and stitches, such as short rows, fair isle, more intricate intarsia, cables, lace patterns, and numerous color changes.

MULTIPLES

Multiples indicate the number of stitches required to form one full repeat of the pattern. We have provided the math for many variations of each pattern in the Customize Your Scarf/Cowl charts. If you wish to branch out to make narrower/wider or shorter/longer versions, do not hesitate to add or subtract stitches in order for your cast on to correspond with the multiple for your chosen pattern. To allow the pattern to work, make sure to add the number (if any) after the multiple to your cast on.

Example: Multiple of 6 + 3 means that you need 6 stitches for each repeat of the pattern plus an extra 3 stitches should be added to the cast on number.

Therefore, 4 repeats of 6 is 24 plus 3 extra stitches = 27 stitches to cast on; 5 repeats of 6 is 30 plus 3 extra stitches = 33 stitches to cast on, 6 repeats of 6 is 36 plus 3 extra stitches = 39 stitches to cast on, and so on.

Gauge **does** have an impact on the size of your project; in order for your Scarf or Cowl to be the size you want, you need to match the gauge given *(see Gauge, page 29).*

DECREASES
KNIT 2 TOGETHER
   (abbreviated K2 tog)

Insert the right needle into the **front** of the first two stitches on the left needle as if to **knit** *(Fig. 1)*, then **knit** them together as if they were one stitch.

Fig. 1

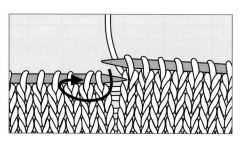

PURL 2 TOGETHER
   (abbreviated P2 tog)

Insert the right needle into the **front** of the first two stitches on the left needle as if to **purl** *(Fig. 2)*, then **purl** them together as if they were one stitch.

Fig. 2

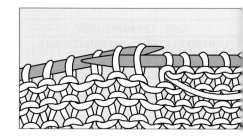

SLIP 1, KNIT 1, PASS SLIPPED STITCH OVER
   (abbreviated slip 1, K1, PSSO)

Slip one stitch as if to **knit**. Knit the next stitch. With the left needle, bring the slipped stitch over the knit stitch *(Fig. 3)* and off the needle.

Fig. 3

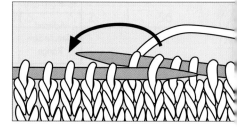

SLIP 1, KNIT 2 TOGETHER, PASS SLIPPED STITCH OVER

(abbreviated slip 1, K2 tog, PSSO)

Slip one stitch as if to **knit**, then knit the next two stitches together *(Fig. 1)*. With the left needle, bring the slipped stitch over the stitch just made *(Fig. 4)* and off the needle.

Fig. 4

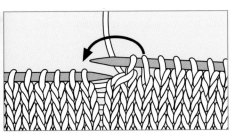

YARN OVER

(abbreviated YO)

after a knit stitch, before a knit stitch

Take the yarn forward **between** the needles, then back **over** the top of the right hand needle, so that it is now in position to knit the next stitch *(Fig. 5a)*.

Fig. 5a

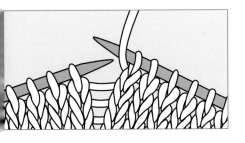

after a purl stitch, before a purl stitch

Take the yarn **over** the right hand needle to the back, then forward **under** it, so that it is now in position to purl the next stitch *(Fig. 5b)*.

Fig. 5b

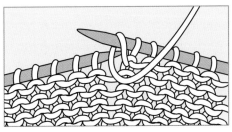

after a purl stitch, before a knit stitch

Take the yarn **over** the right hand needle to the back, so that it is now in position to knit the next stitch *(Fig. 5c)*.

Fig. 5c

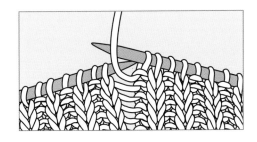

after a knit stitch, before a purl stitch

Take the yarn forward **between** the needles, then back **over** the top of the right hand needle and forward **between** the needles again, so that it is now in position to purl the next stitch *(Fig. 5d)*.

Fig. 5d

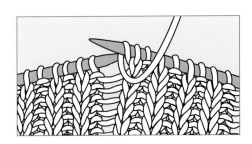

BLOCKING

Blocking helps to smooth your work and give it a professional appearance. Check the yarn label for any special instructions about blocking. With acrylics that can be blocked, place your project on a clean terry towel over a flat surface and pin it in place to the desired size using rust-proof pins where needed. Cover it with dampened bath towels. When the towels are dry, the project is blocked. If the yarn is hand washable, carefully launder your project using a mild soap or detergent. Lay the project on a large towel on a flat surface out of direct sunlight. Gently smooth and pat it to the desired size and shape. When it is completely dry, it is blocked.

Yarn Information

Projects in this book were made using a variety of yarn weights. Any brand of the specified weight of yarn may be used. It is best to refer to the yardage/meters when determining how many balls or skeins to purchase. Remember, to arrive at the finished size, it is the GAUGE/TENSION that is important, not the brand of yarn.

For your convenience, listed below are the specific colors used to create our photography models.

RIBBED
Bernat® Bargello™
Scarf - #43134 Blue
Cowl - #43742 Teal

CLOVER
Red Heart® Boutique™ Treasure™
Scarf - #1923 Tapestry
Cowl - #1918 Abstract

PEBBLES
Premier Yarn® Deborah Norville Collection™
Fashion Jeweltones®
Scarf - #2207 Geode
Cowl - #2201 Moonstone

HALF LINEN
Premier Yarn® Deborah Norville Collection™
Serenity® Sock Solids
Scarf - #5011 Charcoal
Cowl - #5008 Hot Lime

CABLES
Bernat® Vickie Howell Cotton-ish™
Scarf - #85700 Jade Jersey
Cowl - #85628 Cotton Harvest

ZIG ZAG
Caron® Simply Soft® Paints
Scarf - #0002 Rose Garden
Cowl - #0007 Harlequin

We have made every effort to ensure that these instructions are accurate and complete. We cannot, however, be responsible for human error, typographical mistakes, or variations in individual work.

Production Team: Writer/Instructional Editor - Sarah J. Green; Editorial Writer - Susan Frantz Wiles; Senior Graphic Artist - Lora Puls; Graphic Artist - Becca Snider Tally; Photo Stylist - Lori Wenger; and Photographers - Jason Masters and Ken West.